TO GOD BE THE GLORY FOR ALL THE THINGS HE HAS DONE. THANK YOU GOD FOR BLESSING ME, THANK YOU FOR SHINING YOUR LIGHT UPON ME, THANK YOU FOR JUST SIMPLY LOVING ME.

TO MY FAMILY & FRIENDS, I THANK YOU ALL FOR THE SUPPORT, FOR THE LOVE, FOR THE ENCOURAGEMENT. I NEVER THOUGHT THAT I WOULD BE ABLE TO FINISH, BUT YOU ALL KEPT PUSHING ME AND TELLING ME TO NEVER GIVE UP. I DID JUST THAT. I LOVE YOU ALL.

~TEKI

To my Students:

I want you to always remember, anything you set your mind to do you can do it. You guys have pushed me and encouraged me to finish it. Guess what, It is Finished. I encourage you to always stay focused and remember those nuggets I drop during class sometimes.

1. Stay Focused
2. Stay Locked In
3. Remain Humble
4. Get your Education
5. Avoid Negativity
6. Surround yourself around people who mean well
7. Never Give Up
8. Keep Striving for Greatness
9. Go somewhere in Life
10. Go to college & if not get a trade doing something
11. Keep Smiling
12. Keep Loving
13. Keep Grinding
14. Keep Living
15. LOL Don't Forget About Me ;-)

I LOVE YOU ALL

LIVE UNAPOLOGETCTICALLY
LIVE UNASHAMED
LIVE ON PURPOSE

Laugh Uncontrollably
Laugh to feel free
Laughter does good like medicine

LOVE FREELY
LOVE CONQUERS ALL
LOVE UNCONDITIONALLY

TABLE OF CONTENTS
SELF HELP & SELF LOVE

- Loving God
- Loving Self
- Loving Others
- Living
- Laughing
- Life Experiences
- Living on Purpose
- Living in your Now
- Being Healed
- Being Free
- Being You
- Being Healthy
- Expectancy
- Being One
- No Excuses
- Smiling through the Pain
- Winning

CHILDHOOD

Growing up, my family was a normal family with our own issues. We didn't have all of what we wanted, but we had enough to survive. As a child, I went through something I never thought I would experience, seeing my parents go through a divorce. Whewww, that was tough. No child ever want to see their parents hurt, but it happened. I dealt with the broken promises of my Dad, but yet and still I loved him inspite of it all. Through my mom's hurt and the broken promises, my mom, my queen, took good care of my brother and I.

CHILDHOOD

My mother (Yvonne Hankerson), is the most beautifulliest, strongest black woman, I have ever seen. This is where I get my strength and wisdom from. The strength that helps me process and overcome broken promises. I hate it when people say they are going to do something or make a promise and they don't keep it. I HATE IT!, I HATE IT!, I HATE IT! It seem to bring out the little girl inside me that had not healed from broken promises. With the hurt came anger all because my dad broke my heart. Every little girl longs to be daddy's

CHILDHOOD

little girl. Even to this day, I still want that. Over the years, our relationship has gotten better. No one and I mean no one can ever talk bad about him. Even though my dad was not around, my other dad stood in the paint. He took my brother and I in as his own and I thank and love him for that. My mom got her focus back and took care of business and was able to love and live again. I always said that I would never get in a relationship that was like my parents. Boy was I wrong!!! As I got older, I was able to start expressing how I felt with all situations.

YOUNG ADULTHOOD

Years have passed, been in several relationships, saying to myself, I will never be like my parents, I will never date a man like my dad. But I dated a man, that later would disrespect me and do things to hurt me. He cheated on me several times and caused me to go into a deep depression. My life turned upside down in the blink of an eye. I prayed, I cried, I prayed, I cried, and I wanted to not be here anymore. Things just kept going down hill the moment I got out of high school. All I wanted was to just be happy, live life, play basketball, and be successful.

YOUNG ADULTHOOD

People I thought were my friends, weren't: People I thought I could confide in, hurt me! Left not knowing what to do next. I began to put up walls, and felt like I couldn't Trust No One! Back in the older days, people fought to be in relationships even if they were getting hurt in the process, I just didn't want that, but in the end everything I said I didn't want to happen, happened! My mom was so strong, she took, and endured a lot. Just like her, when I love, I love hard and try to do everything to make that person happy, and not choosing me over the disrespect. I allowed those things to happen.

LOVE/RELATIONSHIP

When someone truly cares about you, they will make an effort not and excuse. Secrets and lies kills relationships, and no matter how careful you think you are, you will still get caught eventually Know that what is done in the dark, will always come to light at some point. That happened in my marriage, which ended in divorce. Who would have ever thought, it would happen to me but it did and I had to learn that Life does go on. ~Stay committed to the one you say you love and that loves you back.~

Sometimes, sorry is not enough
*Sometimes you actually have to

LOVE/RELATIONSHIP

change.* When you can't find sunshine, BE the SUNSHINE! When someone loves you, they don't have to say it, you can tell by the way they treat you. My biggest MISTAKE was always thinking "TEAM", while they were thinking "Me or I". Sometimes all you have to do is sit back and observe.

Anyone who wants to be around you, will be around you. Anyone who says they love you, will always show you in action. Anyone who wants to spend time with you, will always make an effort to be there and not give an excuse every time as to why they can't.

LOVE/RELATIONSHIP

**If you are in a relationship, you should NEVER have to beg your partner to see you, to be with you, to call you, to text you, or to love you. It should be a willingness on their part to do to be that person AUTOMATICALLY!!

I think the secret to being happy, is accepting what comes what was, and where you are in life and making the most out of every situation everyday. When you are in a relationship, you want to be happy. You may have ups and downs, but at the end of the day, Love will Conquer All.

LOVING

When you love someone, the very thought of them should make you smile. You like because, and you love despite of. You like someone because of their qualities and you love despite their qualites.

*WHAT IS THE SECRET TO WINNING?

~COMMITMENT, TOTAL COMMITMENT!

WHEN I WIN, WE ALL WIN!

TESTIMONY LIFE LESSON/WORDS OF WISDOM

A few years ago, I almost lost my life. Lying in the hospital bed, not knowing if or whether my plug would be pulled, I just needed to breathe. Life just took an unexpected turn. We have to make life count. When was the last time you took a deep breath? When was the last time you looked at your life? Take a Breath Now! Knowing that no matter what was thrown at you, and knowing that as long as you had breath in your body, you had time to change, to make it worth living for, to make life count, and to live a happy life. Sometimes things happen in our

LIFE LESSON/WORDS OF WISDOM

life, and we don't know why they happen like they do, but we do know that at any moment, we can make a change, we have to keep trusting God. I too have to sit back and just breathe.

Change your perspectives, Change your Mind Process, Avoid Negativity, Speak Life, & Win.
Stop blaming others and deal with your own insecurities. See yourself through the eyes of those who love you. If you love yourself, keep negativity away from your heart. Always Have Positive Vibes and Positive Energy

TESTIMONY/LIFE LESSON

If you don't, It will contaminate you and make you sick. #WISDOM
Always Live your Life to the Fullest

I always use to think, everyone just felt that because I was a strong person, that I didn't have problems or I will get through it, but in reality, I am just a loving and caring soul who was broken inside for a long time. I just wanted someone to fight for me as much as I did for them, love me like I loved them, treat me like I treated them, and not just put my feelings aside until they got

TESTIMONY/LIFE LESSON

ready. I too wanted to be a priority. I always had that from my family and friends, but in a relationship it was always different, but at the end of the day, life went on , and I chose to live life fully. Sometimes we allow fear to cause us to miss what we know is good for us. I have learned that loss is a part of my assignment but Victory is always the purpose, because even when I lose, I Win. Keep living in your Now, and Never give up, & Never allow anyone else to tell you otherwise.

Keep Pushing- Gang!

Live, Grow, & Develop. Stop trying to clear your name or be someone you're not, for people who don't really matter. Don't ever believe you have to be like anybody to be somebody.

NEVER LET A PERSON CHANGE WHO YOU ARE. PRETENDING A PROBLEM DOESN'T EXIST, WILL NOT ONLY EXACERBATE, BUT WILL MAKE A FOOL OUT OF YOU!

*NUGGET-NEVER ALLOW ONE TO MAKE YOU FEEL THAT YOU ARE NOT GOOD ENOUGH, OR YOU ARE NOT A PRIORITY-KEEP MOVING YOU ARE BETTER OFF-TRUST THE PROCESS & TRUST GOD!

LOVE

Lies, willingness to commit disrespect, unprotected, neglected, and other negative behaviors are signs of not being serious about being with that person. Love can't be defined as mere words alone, love is a commitment, love is emotions and not just feelings.

LOVE

When you are in love with someone, that person is the last person you want to see & talk to. Love is not just a word, it is how you show up. Get out of your own way to make room for love in your life & for someone to love you properly.

Nugget

Say it with me, "When you know better, you do better." "Be a better you inspite of the situation that you are going through in your life. Look in the mirror & say, I am Enough, I got this, Nothing can stop me, I will dream again, I will never give up!!"

LIFE LESSON

I had to take a step back and look in the mirror and look at my own reflection and say: "Girl you got this, you are Amazing, No weapon that is formed against you shall prosper, I am a Winner, I am Important".

Do not limit yourself to anything less than what you deserve.

I have learned that people will use you, deplete you, & move on. Know your worth. Life is too short. If you can't let go of your past & see what's in front of you, how can you expect to move forward with your life? Again Trust the Process!

LOVE

The most difficult thing in life that I feel for a friendship or a relationship, is cutting someone out of your life that you love. But helping them is hurting you in the process. You should ask God for strength to help you walk away.

"YOU DESERVE TO BE LOVED THE RIGHT WAY!"
Spend time with the ones who want to spend time with you. Sometimes we as a people feel the need to be broken to feel needed and once that happens and the guard is let down, that is when others seem to push you

LOVE

away so then you end up going back in a shell or in a corner. You then get afraid of losing control and blow shit up before the other person can hurt you, but in reality, not giving the one who truly cares about you a chance before turning and walking away from the person whom my be the best for you. Relationships will never work unless you have commitment, loyalty, trust, establishment, effort, communication, & positive vibes.

Unconditional Love Does Not Mean Unconditional Tolerance

LOVE

Every relationship will get boring if you let it. After being together for years, the newness starts to wear off with time. Not just with relationships, but with cars, new shoe, new games, etc... But Love, Love isn't just a feeling, it is total commitment to love everyday, physically & emotionally. It can be difficult at times because it is not always laughs, smiles, and fun. People tend to quit when it stops being fun and that is when the person starts looking else where. So what are you saying Tequila?

LOVE

"Be the Change You want to see Happen!!" We don't know what tomorrow is going to bring, so always live in the moment. Love doesn't always mean that you agree, see eye to eye, or never have an disagreement. It just simply means that despite the bad days, I still can't see myself without this person. Love is a beautiful thing, when both are willing to be in it, to win it <u>Together!!</u>

LOVE

The only way a person destroys the best things, moments, and relationships in their lives is because they hate who they are, and all the corners in their minds where they keep all the bad stuff, memories & guilt, allows them to not want to face the facts or the circumstances. One will need to look inside all of the corners and take all that stuff out one by one. Take a look at it all for what it is, for what it says about them, and change who they are in their mindset to become a better person.

LOVE
WINNING

*Seek first to understand & then to be understood.

- Recognize the perception of it. Be able to understand someone else's truth.
- Be vulnerable with the one you love.

God does not fix the mess we create. What God can do, will do, and does all the time is give us the courage and presence of mind to do whatever needs to be done to rectify our errors. What we must always do, is ask God for guidance, and trust it will be ok.

TEQUILA'S SECRET TO MAKING A RELATIONSHIP LAST A LIFETIME

*1. Always communicate no matter how tough it gets.
2. Make each other Top Priority
3. Trust must be the Foundation
4. Show affection every single day
5. Don't have arguments, have discussions
6. Speak to understand & comprehend
7. Always go 100 for each other & give it everything up Got
8. Go to God with everything in Prayer and Trust the Process.

NUGGET:

*STOP SWIMMING OCEANS FOR PEOPLE WHO WON'T EVEN CROSS BRIDGES FOR YOU!

*DO THINGS THAT WILL MAKE YOU STAND OUT FROM THE CROWD. BE UNAPOLOGECTIC & LOVE FREELY.
*BE YOURSELF NO MATTER WHAT, BE UNIQUE, LIVE, LEARN, LOVE, & LEAVE A LEGACY!

LOVE

Set goals with your partner, Talk things over, and Stay Committed to One Another. Never give up on your love you have for one another. When you know what you want, you work hard to get it. I am on the verge of finding love again. ;-) You can too! Don't let past relationships, stop you from loving again. It can happen, It will happen, you just have to be open to it. Love Again!

NUGGET

Flesh is a mess on anybody, when we are in pain, we want to cause pain on others, when we are depressed, we want to cause depression on others, but always know that God is in control, continue to trust in him.

NUGGET

HEY YOU,

In case no one has told you lately, I am Proud of You! I am proud of you for pushing through everything you are going through. You are so much stronger than you give yourself credit for and you are Capable of doing anything in this world, I Believe in You & I Love You!!!

REJECTION

Being rejected is hard especially when you know you are a giver and is always there for others. I never wanted to have that feeling of a person telling me NO!. I hated changed. Guess what?, it happened to me on a numerous occasions. The downside of being rejected is that it can put you into a dark place, it can make you become depressed and feeling like you are not worthy despite being there for everyone else. Sometimes it can make you feel like you mean nothing to those people who chooses to push you away. But at the end of the day, I beg you to make peace your priority. Take care of self. Self love is best. Mental Health is Real!

LIFE

When life rearranges itself unexpectedly in front of me, when familiarity and understanding vanishes from beneath, when logic and reason are no longer able to explain away the events unfolding around me. I hold on to the Strength, Hope, & Love inside me. I am more of what I hide than what I show. I keep it inside because that's the safest place to hide. I smile through the pain and never let my guard down. Nothing can break my determination and will to live. I try not to depend on anyone because I know everyone's

LIFE

fighting their own battles and at the end of the day, I have to be my own Hero!

~What's understood, will never have to be explained. If it doesn't challenge you, then it won't change you. Once you have matured, you realize that Silence is more powerful than Proving a Point.

**Sometimes when you love so much and so hard, all you want in return is just for it to be reciprocated.

Real chemistry is rare. Real love is rare. Real is rare. If you ever find it, Keep it!!!

LIFE

~Never assume, it will make an (A-S-S out of U and Me)
~Presumption will lead to disappointment.

~Live enough for today, always live in the moment. Let it be worth the while.

*The road may be difficult at times, but it isn't impossible. Keep Pushing, Keep Grinding!!
*Never let or allow fear to cause you to miss what you know is for you.

Loss is a part, but Victory is always the purpose, even when you lose, you can still Win!

Always love Yourself

LIFE

Life can be tough sometimes, but you got to keep moving forward, keep surrounding yourself around people who are going to push you into your Now and celebrate your Wins. Some of the people who will stress you out sometimes, be the people who are close to you. They know what you're working on & they know what's on your plate. Some people won't care because they will seek out their intereset first & will want you to put yourself on a secondary position. I say that to say this "If you care about me, then care about my time.

LIFE

Throughout life's journey, you may find it hard to be positive sometimes and even though it may seem hard and difficult, it is not impossible.

~Keep Pushing
~Keep Laughing
~Keep Loving
~Keep Living

Time Heals all wounds. Life happens to everyone. "You had a purpose before anyone had an opinion." Some people will only "love you" as much as they can use you. Know who you are!

LIFE

Their loyalty ends where the benefits stop. Choose wisely who you allow to be in your circle and connected to you, because some people only want what they can get & not to see you win. Some people don't mean you no good.

You see my Pastor Bishop Major Callahan (R.I.H.) once said, "people will always be people, meaning, they will talk about you when you do good & they will talk about you when down. You just have to learn how to press forward & do what says the Lord"

LIFE

*One thing is for certain, two things for sure, when I love, I love hard and it takes a lot for me to walk away. I do believe in second chances because people do change, however, understand one thing, if I walk away from you, it's not because I want you to chase me, it's just i'm tired of loving someone to only feel neglected in return, i'm tired of not being viewed as a priority in that persons life, i'm tired of over looking that persons flaws but they continuously nitpick at mine. If I walk away from you, it's not that i'm trying to teach you a lesson, it's I finally understand mine! That's it!! I understand me!! Know that it is ok to not be ok!

LIFE

Sometimes we have to protect ourselves because we are tired of being hurt by the people we knew weren't worth it. Sometimes we are conflicted with compassion and we keep forgiving people who aren't sorry and we keep taking the high road. Scenario: We run out of gas to go pick them up or see them, we get burnt out and nobody appreciates your sacrifice. People are so accustomed to you always being strong, they don't realize or know how to deal with you when you have a weak moment. We will stop everything for a friend in need but the one time we go through it people will act like they are so busy or can't make it. Learn how to suck it up and keep moving.

LIFE

If you ever put me in a situation where you are choosing between me and somebody else, I will say this, I am the type of person where I will make it very easy for you, "*Choose Them*" Because one thing about me is that I will not compete with nobody and I refuse to be a runner up, so with all due respect, I will wish you the best but Remove me as an option.

The older you get, the more you choose calm over chaos and distance over disrespect. Drama becomes intolerable to you and your peace becomes your ultimate priority. You start surrounding yourself with people who are good for your Mental Health, heart, and soul. Self love and care is the best. Choose you over any mess that will keep you stressed.

LIFE

I will never understand why people like wasting other people's time. I don't see why people don't be straight up from the jump, and tell the other person what they really want.

**Like if you just need somebody to talk to, then just say that!!
**Like if you just want somebody that you just want to kick it with and just have fun, then just say that!! (Say Less)
**If you just want someone for what's between their legs, just say that!!
I feel like people in this generation needs to learn how to be more open, vocal, and honest about what they truly want out of a person and to stop wasting people's time. People don't deserve to be lead on thinking that it's going to be something long term when it's really not.

Be honest and tell the truth.

STEPS IN LIVING OR LYING TO YOURSELF

*If you are truly living life to the fullest, you will be truthful and authentic with yourself.

*If you are lying to yourself, you will pretend things are good when they are not.

Step 1: Stop lying to yourself-> It is what is is! Some people are only committed to the brokeness of you (Broke version is very easy to manipulate) because that is when you are the most vulnerable.

*Get around people who will push you into your NOW (Growth). Have a Healthy Mindset.

Step 2: Stop Making Excuses! If they don't ~~see it~~, no matter if you want to see them heal or get better.

*Sometimes for your sanity, you have to leave people in their mess, because if they are not trying to live in peace, disconnect from them.

STEPS IN LIVING OR LYING TO YOURSELF

<u>Step 3</u>: Stop Crying over Missed Moments. Sometimes you invest too much in a relationship. Sometimes you stay in friendships so long that mean you no good. Having an Adult Temper Tantrum, won't change the situation.

*Pick yourself up because you still have Purpose, (It's called a do over day and I still have breath in body to make a change) *As long as you have breath in your body, you have a do over. Give life to everything you speak. Don't dwell on the past because when you do, you will be stuck for the rest of your life.

STOP SELF SABOTAGING YOURSELF!!!

Remain Humble, Stay Focused
&
Live Life on Purpose

STEPS IN LIVING OR LYING TO YOURSELF

STEP 4: GET OUT OF THE NORMAL ROUTINE. WHEN YOU WANT BETTER, YOU DO THE NECESSARY THINGS TO GET BETTER.
-STOP MAKING EXCUSES
-YOU CAN BE UNDERSTANDING DUE TO WHAT WAS IN OTHERS PAST, BUT YOU DON'T HAVE TO EXCEPT THEM TREATING YOU ANY LESS THAN THE BEST. *STOP WAITING ON OTHER PEOPLES APPROVAL! ACCESS AND ADJUST

STEP 5: STAY FOCUSED TO FINISH UNTIL THE MISSION IS COMPLETED/DONE. MAKE UP IN YOUR MIND WHO YOU ARE BEFORE THE HURT, THE PAIN, OR THE FRUSTRATION.
*SPEAK POSITIVITY
*GREATNESS IS IN YOU, STAY FOCUSED!

**Stay the Course, You Got This!!
You deserve to win. Overdue for a Win. Get real about how you will show up for yourself. Have boundaries in your life. Know when to walk away--I can love you and distance myself--I can still love you and still disconnect from you, to keep my peace and sanity.

GOD, FAMILY, LIFE, RELATIONSHIP, FOCUS

You can never make yourself happy bringing misery to other people. Sometimes to see the rainbow, you have to put up with a little rain. It takes wisdom, it takes maturity, and it takes restraint to deal with trifling, negative, and fake people.

~Important people come and go, that's ok
~Look at is as rejection or redirection
~You define what fun is, and don't let anyone say what you like is stupid.
~Sometimes you have to let other people down to make yourself happy and to avoid negative vibes.

~Stop trying to prove your point to people who already made their mind up about you. Learn to peep, understand, and fall back for your protection and safety.

GOD, FAMILY, LIFE, RELATIONSHIP, FOCUS

~TRAIN YOUR MIND TO BE STRONGER THAN YOUR EMOTIONS OR ELSE YOU WILL LOSE YOURSELF EVERY TIME.
~LIVE EVERY MOMENT, LAUGH EVERYDAY, AND LOVE BEYOND MEASURES UNCONDITIONALLY.

Life Lesson: If you ever feel like you don't want to be with that person, let them know, because if you don't you both will be hurt in the end. You should never cheat or lie to your partner. You tell one lie then you will have to cover up that lie with another. Why they Lie! Why they Lie!

*The difference in needing and wanting someone is that when I need you~I can't survive if I don't have you, then the need turns into spiritually, mentally, you have my heart and soul and now it's not tangible things. When I want you~it's a choice ~making a choice to be with you.

GOD, FAMILY, LIFE, RELATIONSHIP, FOCUS

~When you go through life, many obstacles can be thrown in your path to stop you, to detour you, to turn you around, but you have to stay strong and endure to the end. When you have no one to encourage you, Encourage yourself, "I can & I will make it"

DAILY PRAYER

I WOKE UP
I AM BREATHING
MY LEGS ARE MOVING
MY HEART IS BEATING
MY FUTURE IS BRIGHT
WHAT MORE CAN I SAY?
THAN YOU LORD FOR
THE SMALL MERCIES & FAVOR
I SEE EVERYDAY.

YOU GOT TO HEAL YOURSELF FIRST

You will not be able to determine who you need in your life, until you are able to fill your own void. You'll choose someone out of your pain and then when you get well, you don't want them anymore. "Its almost like marrying a nurse". You're attracted to them because you are sick and they are good at making you feel better, you have no purpose for them in your life and all of a sudden you say you have outgrown them ~No you haven't outgrown them, you just built a world around your affliction.

*BE HEALED FROM YOUR PAIN *BE FREE FROM YOUR MIND *BE YOU ALWAYS

TESTIMONY #2

For many years, since 2006, I have dealt with fibroids. Fibroids are uterine myomas that are noncancerous growths in the uterus that can develop unexpectedly. It is most in African American women Even though they are noncancerous, they can cause a lot of other problems, and in my case it did. I was first diagnosed with fibroids in 2006. I didn't know what it was, I just knew I had two of them, one the size of a nickel and the other the size of a dime. I suffered from heavy bleeding, clots, iron deficiency, tiredness, depression a little, and the asking of questions of Why Me?? Six years later, those two fibroids had grown into two big grapefruits. Big I know right! I started to have pain in my lower abdomen and in my lower back. I went to my Gynecologist and when you live in a small town, you tend to not have all the resources available. Well, my Gynecologist at the time said to me

TESTIMONY #2

you have two options, first option is I can put you on birth control to see if it can dissolve them or second option is we can do a hysterectomy. At the time of my age, I said we will not be doing the second option because I do want to have kids some day. Again, lack of resources, so when the resources are not there, they don't share all of the information because they still want you to come to them. Shaking my head, I contacted a friend of mine at the time who lived in Orlando and said to me come up here and see my doctor to get a second opinion. Me, "Say Less". I went to see this doctor and in talking with him, I felt comfortable and he gave me other options. Wheww!!! I said ok lets make it happen. So on May of 2012 I had a surgery called Myomectomy, which is where they go in orthroscopy robotically to remove the fibroids. Long rode to recovery.

TESTIMONY #2

After recovery, out here living my best life, thinking okay they are gone, I can be pain free, not have to worry about bleeding as much. Well, I was hit with a slap in the face again. I started to have dizzy spells, low iron, bleeding for 3 months straight, had to have a blood transfusion, I was in and out of the hospitals and doctor offices, IV's, and guess what they came back!! ☹

I said to myself, "Here we go again." On March 20, 2017 I was in the hospital having surgery at Winnie Palmer Hospital in Orlando, FL. I was taken back that morning about 7:00 am. The doctor came to my mother at around 2:00 pm and told her that I was in recovery and everything went okay and that she would be able to see me within an hour. Well, in that time, the doctor came back to my mother and said these words, "I am sorry we will have to go back in because she is bleeding out.

TESTIMONY #2

I was really about to leave this place. What happened was when they rushed to put the tube back down my throat, they scraped my throat and it swole up around the tube so they couldn't remove it, my mom and friend were finally able to see me at around 10:30-11:00 pm. When they saw me in ICU, I was on the ventilator heavily sedated.

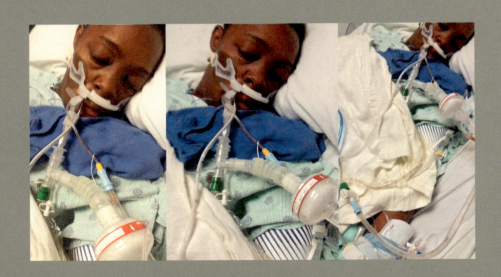

TESTIMONY #2

Over the next few days, it was very challenging. the ups, the downs, infections, and everything that could go wrong, did, I would then spend the next 9 days in the ICU and 5 days on a ventilator and by the way, no one that is on a ventilator should be awake, it was horrible. I felt like I couldn't breathe and became very anxious and agitated. I spend the next 3 days on a different floor after I got out of ICU. I said to these people are trying to kill me, I am ready to go home. I had a long road to recovery.

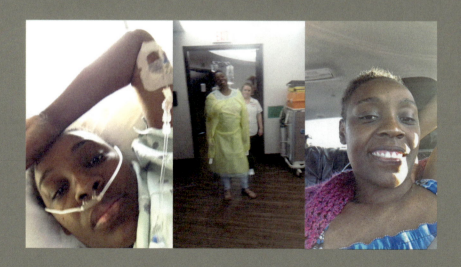

TESTIMONY #2

3 months later, I started to get back to myself again. Time waits for no one. I said okay, I have time now, everything is back to normal and I will now be able to have a baby just to find out that the fibroids came back again. At this point I am angry, because I am like why me, why do I have to keep going through this. Uggghhhhh!!!! And on March 8, 2022, I find myself back in Winnie Palmer Hospital to find out I will be having a complete hysterectomy with no chance of being able to have kids out of my body. ☹

I was really sick and was just living my life not knowing how bad it really was. Thank God for his covering and my mom, family, and friends prayers. This by far was a hard pill to swallow. Again, time waits for no one. I said all of that to say this, "You never know what life will throw at you, it's okay to ask why, but you also need to be in a place where you can receive the answer

TESTIMONY #2

you have been searching for. God gives his strongest tasks to his strongest soldiers, at the moment, I didn't know I was one of them, but through it all I made it out okay. Continue to Trust God process for your life, you may not understand it, and that's okay, keep pushing, keep praying, and keep moving. I didn't understand why I wouldn't be able to bear children, but as I reflect, I know that there are a lot of children who are in need of a family that are in the system. That's my plan in the future, to become a mom of my own child. Through my journey, I've learned a whole lot. A question that was asked to me before, "What profit is it for man to gain the whole world and lose his soul?" Is it worth it? Is it worth living for other people. My opinion, No, you have to keep your circle small and get with people that's going to pray, push,

TESTIMONY #2

and elevate you. We have to know who we are and whose we are. We have to learn how to push pass people and live life to the fullest on purpose, love wholeheartedly, and love so unconditionally, and pray for those that despitefully use you.

Listen I had to learn and you can too, it may always seem impossible until its done and if you need help please don't be afraid to ask.

Through my journey, I've also realized that God gives his toughest trials to his strongest because what's important afterwards is what matters the most, unlocking those keys to help and teach to someone else.

BE YOU ALWAYS

BE FREE

BE UNIQUE

BE UNAPOLOGETIC

KEEP GOD FIRST & YOU WILL ALWAYS WIN

Make a promise to yourself to stay true to yourself and never compromise your values for anyone or anything else ever again.

It's time to focus on you, get you back, love on yourself, be good to you! Once you get your focus back on the things that matter, everything else will fall right in place. Keep trusting God to guide you in the right direction. Don't allow others to dictate your life. I said it before and I will say it again, Self Love is the Best Love. Then and only then, you will be able to except love from others.

JUST STAY FOCUSED!!

THANK YOU

I would like to take the time to thank God for everything. You have definitely blown my mind over this project. I would like to thank my parents for always supporting me and loving me in spite of and also encouraging me to move forward. I would like to thank my brother for supporting me and pushing me to do great things. I want to thank my special friend for always having my back, supporting me, encouraging me to write again, to pick this pen up to finish my book, for listening to me. I want to thank all my family and friends for your support. I also want to thank all the people of who I have had the pleasure to come in contact with, whether it was a friendship, relationship, family, haters, etc. It is because of you all that I was able to write this book, to encourage others to keep pressing, to keep moving forward, to keep loving hard,

THANK YOU

to keep laughing and smiling no matter what, to keep praying, and to keep living your best life. So Thank You All from the Bottom of my Heart.

Signed, Your Favorite Write & Encourager

Tequila L. Rouse

IN MEMORY OF MALIK KAHLIL PEARSON

July 14, 2009 - May 15, 2023

YOU WERE TAKEN FROM US TOO SOON, YOUR MEMORIES WILL LIVE IN OUR HEARTS FOREVER!

GONE BUT NEVER FORGOTTEN

#LLM

In remembrance of my Grandma Virginia McGahee and Lottie Mae Mckinnie, I love and miss you both. I know that you would be so proud of me.

....

....

....

....

....

NOTE TO SELF
....
Today will be
a good day

....

....

....

....

....

NOTE TO SELF
....
Today will be
a good day
....

....

....

....

....

....

NOTE TO SELF
....
Today will be
....
a good day

GOAL
Getter

....

....

....

....

....

NOTE TO SELF
....

Today will be a good day

....

....

....

....

....

NOTE TO SELF
....
Today will be
a good day

NOTE TO SELF

Today will be a good day

....

....

....

....

....

NOTE TO SELF
....
Today will be
a good day
....

....

....

....

....

....

NOTE TO SELF
....
Today will be
....
a good day

....

....

....

....

....

NOTE TO SELF
....
Today will be
a good day

....

....

....

....

....

NOTE TO SELF
....
Today will be a good day
....

NOTE TO SELF

Today will be a good day

....

....

....

....

....

NOTE TO SELF
....
Today will be
a good day

....

....

....

....

....

NOTE TO SELF
....
Today will be
....
a good day

....

....

....

....

....

NOTE TO SELF
....
Today will be
a good day
....

Made in the USA
Columbia, SC
15 February 2025

53859943R00044